Machines with Power!

Race Cars

by Amy McDonald

BELLWETHER MEDIA
MINNEAPOLIS, MN

Blastoff! Beginners are developed by literacy experts and educators to meet the needs of early readers. These engaging informational texts support young children as they begin reading about their world. Through simple language and high frequency words paired with crisp, colorful photos, Blastoff! Beginners launch young readers into the universe of independent reading.

Blastoff! Universe ★

Reading Level

Grade K

Grades 1-3

Grade 4

Sight Words in This Book 🔍

a	down	make	they
and	go	on	this
are	here	sit	to
at	is	that	up
can	it	the	
do	look	these	

This edition first published in 2022 by Bellwether Media, Inc.

No part of this publication may be reproduced in whole or in part without written permission of the publisher. For information regarding permission, write to Bellwether Media, Inc., Attention: Permissions Department, 6012 Blue Circle Drive, Minnetonka, MN 55343.

Library of Congress Cataloging-in-Publication Data

Names: McDonald, Amy, author.
Title: Race cars / by Amy McDonald.
Description: Minneapolis, MN : Bellwether Media, Inc., 2022. | Series: Blastoff! Beginners : Machines with power! | Includes bibliographical references and index. | Audience: Ages 4-7 | Audience: Grades K-1 |
Identifiers: LCCN 2021003772 (print) | LCCN 2021003773 (ebook) | ISBN 9781644874790 (library binding) | ISBN 9781648343872 (ebook)
Subjects: LCSH: Automobiles, Racing--Juvenile literature.
Classification: LCC TL236 .M3744 2022 (print) | LCC TL236 (ebook) | DDC 629.228/5--dc23
LC record available at https://lccn.loc.gov/2021003772
LC ebook record available at https://lccn.loc.gov/2021003773

Editor: Christina Leaf   Designer: Andrea Schneider

Printed in the United States of America, North Mankato, MN.

Table of Contents

What Are Race Cars?

Vrooom!
Look at that
race car go!

Race cars are
fast machines.
They race to win!

6

Parts of a Race Car

This is the **engine**. It makes the car go.

engine

These are
the tires.
They **grip**
the road.

tire

This is the **cockpit**. The driver sits here.

cockpit

This is the seat.
It keeps
the driver safe.
Buckle up!

seat

Race Cars at Work

Stock cars drive on tracks. They do **laps**.

stock car

track

Rally cars drive on roads. They can go on dirt and snow!

rally car

Dragsters race down a line. Ready...GO!

dragster

Race Car Facts

Race Car Parts

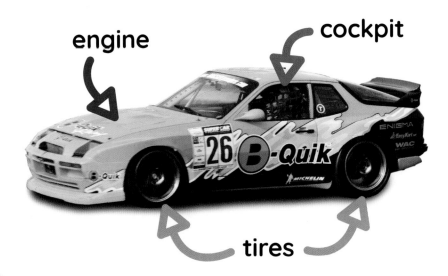

engine

cockpit

tires

Types of Race Cars

stock car

rally car

dragster

Glossary

cockpit

a place for
the driver

engine

the part that
makes a car go

grip

to grab or hold

laps

trips around
a track

To Learn More

ON THE WEB

FACTSURFER

Factsurfer.com gives you a safe, fun way to find more information.

1. Go to www.factsurfer.com.

2. Enter "race cars" into the search box and click 🔍.

3. Select your book cover to see a list of related content.

Index

The images in this book are reproduced through the courtesy of: Hedley Lamarr, front cover; Matthew Jacques, p. 3; Dmitry Feoktistov/ Getty, pp. 4-5; tuaindeed, p. 6; Photomdp, pp. 6-7; Al Mueller, p. 8; Steve Bruckmann, pp. 8-9; renkshot, p. 10; efecreata.com, pp. 10-11; burnel1, p. 12; Grindstone Media Group, pp. 12-13, 16-17, 23 (laps); Alvey & Towers Picture Library/ Alamy, p. 14; Fabio Pagani, pp. 14-15, 23 (cockpit); oneinchpunch, p. 16; Fayzulin Serg, p. 18; EvrenKalinbacak, pp. 18-19; Evgenyrychko, p. 20; Bruce Alan Bennett, pp. 20-21, 22 (dragster); sippakorn, p. 22 (race car parts); action sports, p. 22 (stock car); Mikael Hjerpe, p. 22 (rally car); Ron Frank, p. 23 (engine); Stephen Coburn, p. 23 (grip).